THE RISE OF THE INTERCESSORS

The Rise of the Intercessors
© 2022

Scripture quotations are from The Holy Bible,
New International Version (NIV) unless otherwise stated.

Authors contact details:
Email: ansydessources@yahoo.com
Website: www.ansydessources.com

ISBN: 979-8-9862387-0-8

Published by

Ansy Dessources

Table of Contents

PROLOGUE

The Heart of an Intercessor

During these last days, it's imperative for the people of God to start a godly revolution that will awaken the souls of humanity. There is a great need for a shift in the body of Christ from being rooted in the world to a greater and deeper awareness of the kingdom and what God wants to do through each of us. As our hearts shift and align more and more with the purposes of God, we are able to impact the world around us. A key component of this revolution will consist of intercession-kingdom intercessors must arise!

To *intercede* means *to intervene* on behalf of another. Through intercession, a believer steps in and fills gaps by inviting God to move in families, communities, nations, and individual situations. Intercession helps bring reconciliation among enemies and can prevent damaging and dangerous things from happening. It can also be defined as intermediation, negotiation, and intervention. Simply put, it's the action of praying on behalf of another person or persons.[1]

Intercession is needed more than ever, and believers from every corner of the world must gather to pray wholeheartedly. We need radical prophetic intercession that will change the very global situation that we are going through right now, as intercession can prevent things like wars, crises within families, and poverty, among many other things.

We Need to Learn How to Intercede!

The purpose of this book is to help raise up intercessors in the body of Christ. We want to teach you how to yield and position yourself so God can build you into an intercessor who carries His heart. We will be looking at key intercessors and what we can learn from their lives and experiences.

Abraham

In Genesis 18:16-33, Abraham negotiates with God for his nephew, Lot. This is one of the most commonly used passages on intercession. Yet, as we will discover, there are many key details about intercession in this story that aren't often discussed.

Moses

Both Exodus 32:11-14 and Psalm 106:23 share a similar story of Moses standing in the gap for the children of Israel. Moses is a great example of an intercessor because he interceded for his enemies. Moses pleaded with God for Pharaoh, a man who was enslaving his people (Exodus 8:8-31).

Samuel

We can also glean a lot from how Samuel interceded for the nation of Israel (1 Samuel 3-8). Samuel could have had plenty of excuses not to be a good intercessor, yet he overcame all the odds and became an example of a *true* intercessor. Samuel also had a very important perspective about intercession, as revealed in 1 Samuel 12:23: "Moreover, as for me, far be it from me that I should sin against the LORD by ceasing to pray for you, and I will instruct you in the good and the right way."

Jesus, the Greatest Intercessor

Jesus is the perfect intercessor because His intercession goes beyond the grave. He is currently interceding for us, even while in Heaven (John 17:20-23; Hebrews 7:23-26).

When the Intercessors Pray Wholeheartedly

Intercessors are like brooms or vacuums that cleanse the home of dirt. As a person intercedes on behalf of an individual, family, community, city, county, state, nation, and the world, God moves to purge evil and bring alignment in these areas. Through prayers of intercession, many lives and situations are positively changed by the power and influence of God.

Sin has created a gap between God and man. As one intercedes, they become a bridge that connects the world to God. As Saint Augustine said, "Without God, man cannot, and without man, God will not."

The disciples once asked Jesus to teach them how to pray. Luke 11:1 says that as Jesus was praying, "...one of his disciples said to him, 'Lord, teach us to pray, just as John taught his disciples'". He will teach us how to intercede, as He taught His disciples so long ago.

Let us pray!

INTRODUCTION

I've discovered that many believers today have no idea how to intercede on behalf of others. I've seen many believers respond in criticism and judgment when their own brothers and sisters in Christ share their mishaps and failures. Covering them is what we're actually called to do, especially in prayer. Someone once said that the reason God allows individuals to know about someone else's mistakes or weaknesses is to make a difference in that person's life.

In Jonah 3, we read about the King of Nineveh's intercession for his people.

> "When Jonah's warning reached the king of Nineveh, he rose from his throne, took off his royal robes, covered himself with sackcloth and sat down in the dust. This is the proclamation he issued in Nineveh: 'By the decree of the king and his nobles: Do not let people or animals, herds or flocks, taste anything; do not let them eat or drink. But let people and animals be covered with sackcloth. Let everyone call urgently on God. Let them give up their evil ways and their violence. Who knows? God may yet relent and with compassion turn from his fierce anger so that we will not perish.' When God saw what they did and how they turned from their

evil ways, he relented and did not bring on them the destruction he had threatened" (Jonah 3:6-10).

After hearing that judgment was pronounced by God over his city, the King of Nineveh responded by having his whole nation humble themselves and intercede. He had everyone and everything fast for three days, including the animals in the land. God heard their cries and did not destroy Nineveh (Jonah 3:6-10).

God really listens to the heart of intercessors when they're pleading their cause before God. However, I've noticed over the years that even intercessors are often slow to respond like the King of Nineveh and cry out to God. Because of this, things like sex trafficking, racism, drugs, hatred, alcoholism, gangs, wars, divorce, sexual immorality, poverty, and things of this nature are allowed to continue and grow in the earth (1 Timothy 2:1-4).

Instead of praying, we are often too busy being offended as Jonah was. The prophet Jonah was upset because he wanted to see God destroy Nineveh. He was too offended by how evil the people of Nineveh were to celebrate the fact that God had a plan to restore them (Jonah 4).

Believers must not allow offense to distract them from being the priests that God has called them to be. Peter states, "But you are a chosen race, a royal priesthood, a holy nation, a people for his own possession, that you may proclaim the excellencies of him who called you out of darkness into his marvelous light" (1 Peter 2:9 ESV). As members of the royal priesthood, it is our responsibility to offer prayers that will help forward the will of God on earth and cause others to be brought out of darkness into marvelous light.

God does not want to destroy the world- He wants to restore it. This is why He looks for people to stand in the gap.

> "I looked for someone among them who would build up the wall and stand before me in the gap on behalf of the land so I would not have to destroy it, but I found no one (Ezekiel 22:30).

God is looking for intercessors who will show up in prayer with a heart full of passion to fight in prayer for individuals, families, communities, cities, counties, states, nations and the whole world. When churches have prayer meetings, we should do what we can to attend!

Rise to Fight on Behalf of Others

You are praying for a generation that is facing possibly the most difficult cultural landscape in history. The whole world is in a deep sleep right now, spiritually speaking. I believe a large part of this is due to technology, which can serve as a great blessing but has also become a stumbling block.

According to a study of 11,000 people, RescueTime found that people spend around three hours and fifteen minutes a day on the phone. Most people check their phones about fifty-eight times a day, with thirty of those times taking place during work hours[2] .

It's great for you to use technology and to find great opportunities from it, but God ought to be glorified in everything that we're a part of. God has given us freedoms and rights, yet we must not conclude that we can just do anything we want, as if our actions are inconsequential. Paul once elaborated on this concept of "freedoms and rights" when he explained to the church in Corinth about the fact that having rights doesn't mean everything is right to do because we must not be mastered by anything.

> "'I have the right to do anything,' you say—but not everything is beneficial. 'I have the right to do anything'—but I will not be mastered by anything" (1 Corinthians 6:12).

Prayer warriors cannot afford to be distracted by technology. Warriors need to rise in order to intercede on behalf of those who are lost and those who are in a deep sleep. We must seek and save the lost like Jesus did, and this starts with us praying like Jesus did (Luke 19:9-10; Hebrews 5:7).

It is a warrior's responsibility to stand in the gap so that humanity can be driven back to the altar and prosper at the same time. The world is at the precipice of prophecy; the end times are advancing rapidly. Intercession will open many people's eyes, change hearts, and glorify God!

CHAPTER 1

The Heart of God

When someone desires to grow to be a true intercessor, that person must inevitably answer this question: *what is the heart of God like?* A true intercessor must always be in a place of both being in touch with and learning how to carry the heart of God.

As I spent time in prayer on this topic, I felt led to study the Ark of the Covenant. I looked at how it was designed, and through this, the Holy Spirit began to reveal to me different aspects of the heart of God.

After God delivered the Israelites from being enslaved by the Egyptians, He led them to Mount Sinai. There, He gave Moses specific instructions on how to build the Ark of the Covenant and the Tent of Meeting. The Ark of the Covenant was built to temporarily carry the presence of God, and the Tent of Meeting was the place where the priests would meet on special occasions with God on the behalf of the people of Israel (Exodus 12-34, Leviticus 16:29; Hebrews 5:1-5; Hebrews 9).

We can learn a lot about God's heart by taking a closer look at what He commands to be placed in the Ark of the Covenant. The Bible says,

> "And he made two cherubim of gold. He made them of hammered work on the two ends of the mercy seat, one cherub on the one end, and one cherub on the other end. Of one piece with the mercy seat he made the cherubim on its two ends. The cherubim spread out their wings above, overshadowing the mercy seat with their wings, with their faces one to another; toward the mercy seat were the faces of the cherubim."
> (Exodus 37: 7-9 ESV)

The mercy seat that the two angelic cherubim overshadowed while facing each other was the lid of the Ark of the Covenant, known as the Atonement Cover. Inside the Ark was the Ten Commandments, a golden jar with manna in it, and Aaron's rod that had budded (Exodus 16:34; Numbers 17:10; Hebrews 9:4). Each of these items can be viewed as symbols for the Godhead.

The Ten Commandments are connected to God the Father who gives us the Law to reveal his standard of absolute righteousness (Romans 3:19-20). They were written by the finger of God Himself twice on tablets of stone, indicating their eternal nature (Exodus 31:18; Deuteronomy 9:10). Aaron's rod that budded and grew fruit without it being planted (Number 17:8) shadows the work of the Holy Spirit, who helps us grow fruit in our lives (Galatians 5:22-23).

Furthermore, it was meant to be a sign to the rebellious (Numbers 17:10). Likewise, the Holy Spirit is a sign to the world that they are in rebellion, and it convicts them of sin (John 16:8). Lastly, the manna signifies Jesus Christ, who was the true bread that came from Heaven (John 6:50-52).

The mercy seat covers all the elements in the Ark of the Covenant. James said, "For judgment is without mercy to one who has shown no mercy. Mercy triumphs over judgment" (James 2:13 ESV). The statement that mercy triumphs or is victorious over judgment implies that if there were to be a battle between mercy and judgment, mercy would always prevail.

God designed the Ark of the Covenant the way He did to reveal who He is: a God whose heart is full of mercies and who prefers that judgment would never precede mercy. When the priests or Moses would show up to the Tent of Meeting, God would appear to them, in a cloud of glory, above the mercy seat between the two cherubim Moses would hear him speak (Exodus 25:22; Numbers 7:89; Isaiah 37:16). Once a year on Yom Kippur, the Day of Atonement, the high priest would enter into the Holy of Holies where the Ark of the Covenant was kept and intercede on the behalf of the Israelites.

He would sprinkle the sacrificial blood of the lamb that was slain for the sins of the nation of Israel on the mercy seat. This foreshadowed what Jesus would do when He became a ransom for our sin.

> "But when Christ appeared as a high priest of the good things that have come, then through the greater and more perfect tent (not made with hands, that is, not of this creation) he entered once for all into the holy places, not by means of the blood of goats and calves but by means of his own blood, thus securing an eternal redemption. For if the blood of goats and bulls, and the sprinkling of defiled persons with the ashes of a heifer, sanctify for the purification of the flesh, how much more will the blood of Christ, who through the eternal Spirit offered himself without blemish to God, purify our conscience from dead works to serve the living God" (Hebrews 9:11-14 ESV).

When Jesus died, He entered the perfect tent (which is Heaven) and His blood was sprinkled symbolically on the mercy seat of God the Father's throne. Through selflessly sacrificing Himself, Jesus appeased the wrath of God for the whole world (1 John 2:1-3). This does not mean God wasn't full of mercies before Jesus came-it's actually evident that He was and is full of mercy because He did this after bearing with humanity for centuries.

David attests throughout the Old Testament that God is full of mercies as well as loving and compassionate. Therefore, when Jesus Christ displayed through His life the mercy of God, He manifested what had always been on God's heart. Paul calls this the "mystery of His will," which is that God, since creation, had always desired in His heart that the world would be restored (Ephesians 1-6).

Anyone who comes to God and never realizes that God is loving has yet to truly come to God. For the Bible says this about God:

> "Beloved, let us love one another, for love is from God, and whoever loves has been born of God and knows God. Anyone who does not love does not know God, because God is love. In this the love of God was made manifest among us, that God sent his only Son into the world, so that we might live through him. In this is love, not that we have loved God but that he loved us and sent his Son to be the propitiation for our sins" (1 John 4:7-10 ESV).

John makes it clear here that it was God who loved the world, and because of His love for the world, He sent His

Son. Jesus came first and foremost because God loved the world and had mercy on it! And if anyone does not walk in this love, they do not know God because God is love.

To walk in this love that John spoke about, we must realize that the Ark of the Covenant was actually not God's desired dwelling place. *God wanted to dwell in our hearts.* For God spoke through Jeremiah and Ezekiel about how one day He would inscribe His law on our hearts (Jeremiah 31:33-34; Ezekiel 11:19; Ezekiel 36:26). The inscription of the law on our hearts can be likened to the inscription of the law on the tablets of stone.

> "And I will give you a new heart, and a new spirit I will put within you. And I will remove the heart of stone from your flesh and give you a heart of flesh. And I will put my Spirit within you and cause you to walk in my statutes and be careful to obey my rules" (Ezekiel 36:26-27 ESV).

When Jesus came, He brought about the new heart, spirit, and the inscription of the law on our hearts that God had prophesied through Ezekiel.

Jesus said,

> "'If you love me, keep my commands. And I will ask the Father, and he will give you another advocate to help you and be with you forever— the Spirit of truth. The world cannot accept him,

because it neither sees him nor knows him. But you know him, for he lives with you and will be in you…Anyone who loves me will obey my teaching. My Father will love them, and we will come to them and make our home with them'" (John 14:15-17; John 14:23).

In this passage you can see how God the Father, God the Son and God the Holy Spirit-the trinity-make their dwelling in us when we choose to obey the commands of Jesus. Specifically, the trinity will dwell in our hearts after we welcome Jesus into our lives. The dwelling of the trinity in our hearts parallels the Ten Commandments, Aaron's rod that budded, and the manna that was placed in the Ark of the Covenant.

Paul further elaborates on this concept of us being a dwelling place of God when he says, "Do you not know that your bodies are temples of the Holy Spirit, who is in you, whom you have received from God? You are not your own; you were bought at a price. Therefore, honor God with your bodies" (1 Corinthians 6:19-20). According to Paul, we are God's temple. Just as the temple in the Old Testament housed the Ark of the Covenant, the believer's body now has become a home for the Spirit of God.

The temple in the Old Testament had three specific areas: the outer courts, the inner courts, and the Holy of

Holies (1 Kings 6:36; Jeremiah 35:4; Jeremiah 36:10; Ezekiel 8:16; 2 Chronicles 4:9). The Ark of the Covenant dwelt in the Holy of Holies.

Likewise, our bodies also have three parts. When speaking to the church in Thessalonica, Paul states, "May God himself, the God of peace, sanctify you through and through. May your whole spirit, soul and body be kept blameless at the coming of our Lord Jesus Christ" (1 Thessalonians 5:23). In this farewell prayer, Paul addresses three parts of our body: spirit, soul, and body. Our bodies would be the same as the outer courts, our souls the inner courts, and our spirit (or heart) the holy of holies, the place where the triune God dwells.

Since our hearts, when we are in Christ, are similar to the Ark of the Covenant, mercy should triumph over judgment in us in every area of our lives, including when we intercede for others. It is clear from the Old Testament to the New Testament that God is slow to anger and quick to forgive our sins. As David says in the Psalm, "But you, Lord, are a compassionate and gracious God, slow to anger, abounding in love and faithfulness" (Psalms 86:15).

So, what is the heart of God like? The heart of God is loving, filled with mercies, and full of compassion. And our loving God wants us to have the same kind of heart.

Jude writes, ""Be merciful to those who doubt; save others by snatching them from the fire; to others show mercy, mixed with fear—hating even the clothing stained by corrupted flesh" (Jude 1:22-23). This verse is one that every intercessor should memorize.

When we pray for a world that is lost it should flow from a merciful heart-a heart like God's.

CHAPTER 1 QUESTIONS

1. Explain what it means to know the heart of God.

2. Our bodies are a _____ of God.

3. According to the author, if there were a battle between mercy and judgment, _____ would prevail.

4. When we pray for a lost world, we should have a _____ heart.

5. What can you do to cultivate the heart of God within yourself?

CHAPTER 2

The Revealed Will of God

Alongside learning and carrying God's heart, intercessors must know and settle in their hearts what God's will is, especially regarding key issues. By doing so, an intercessor can potentially save much time and effort that's often wasted by praying from a place of uncertainty.

And can we know what God's will is? *By what He's revealed in His Word.*

For instance, people know that God is love, and that He loves people. However, when someone gets sick and is suffering, many often plead with God to heal that person with a heart of ambiguity, hoping that God will heal them but not really sure if He's willing to. I've found that while people believe God can heal, they don't often think He will unless they "wrestle" with Him in prayer long enough for Him to finally release healing.

When you pray this way, *you are still uncertain of the heart of God* because part of knowing His heart is knowing His will-what has He already revealed to be His desire toward humanity? As we'll look at in this chapter, when it pertains to healing, His desire is that humans be whole.

When you pray from a position of knowing His revealed will, you've already settled in your heart that it's God's intention, for instance, for people to be well. You don't have to waver or wonder if the person is even supposed to get healed at all-you can stand on God's promises and ask Holy Spirit for wisdom on how to pray-but you don't have to wonder if God wants to heal that person.

Now obviously, there will be situations where you're not sure of what the will of God is, and that's perfectly fine! That's why we have access to the mind of God through the Spirit of God (1 Corinthians 2:11, Romans 8:27). The Holy Spirit knows the perfect will of the Father, and when an intercessor prays in the Spirit, God gives insight and direction on how to pray.

In John 5:19, Jesus said that He can only do "what He sees His Father doing" and that "whatever the Father does, the Son also does". Likewise, in John 4:34 Jesus said that He did not come to do His will, but the will of the Father.

Therefore, we can conclude that whatever Jesus did in His ministry on the earth **is the revealed will of God for humanity.**

So what did Jesus do that reveals God's will? Let's look at a few things that are the will of God, as evidenced by the life, ministry, and teachings of Jesus, as well as other places throughout Scripture:

Healing

So much of Jesus' ministry involved healing, and it's important for an intercessor to know that God actually desires for us to be whole. In fact, He so desires this that He made it available through the death and resurrection of Jesus.

Isaiah 53:4 states that "He bore our sicknesses and carried our diseases in His body on the cross". This Old Testament prophecy became a New Testament reality when Jesus began to cast demons out of people and heal them.

> "When evening came, many who were demon-possessed were brought to him, and he drove out the spirits with a word and **healed all the sick.** This was to fulfill what was spoken through the prophet

Isaiah: 'He took up our infirmities and bore our diseases'" (Matthew 8:16-18).

There are many other instances where Jesus freely healed people, clearly revealing God's desire to heal. Thus, when we pray or intercede for someone who is sick, it's important that we align heart with the truth that God's will is to heal.

Prosperity

To be prosperous is to be successful, and success is not just limited to the financial realm. God wants us to prosper in every way-mentally, emotionally, spiritually, relationally, physically, and yes, even financially.

However, the body of Christ is typically divided on the topic of financial prosperity. Many scoff at the idea, making the argument that to be prosperous is self-serving and not heavenly-minded. Many think that poverty is the way to true holiness because it forces you to be in a position where you depend on God.

There are obviously those who are excessive and indulgent with finances, purchasing things they could probably do without and being lavish. That's why the great middle ground is the Word of God. Regardless of perspective, *what has God revealed to be His will regarding prosperity?* Let's take a look at some Scriptures:

Deuteronomy 8:18
But remember the Lord your God, for it is he who gives you the ability to produce wealth, and so confirms his covenant, which he swore to your ancestors, as it is today.

Jeremiah 29:11
"For I know the plans I have for you," declares the Lord. "Plans to prosper you and not to harm you, plans to give you a hope and a future."

Proverbs 10:22
The blessing of the Lord brings wealth, without painful toil for it.

Psalm 1:1-3
Blessed is the one who does not walk in step with the wicked or stand in the way that sinners take or sit in the company of mockers, but whose delight is in the law of the Lord, and who meditates on his law day and night. That person is like a tree planted by streams of water, which yields its fruit in season and whose leaf does not wither-whatever they do prospers.

Clearly, it is the will of the Father for us to prosper in all ways, and this fully realized as we submit to Him and yield to the working of the Holy Spirit in our hearts.

Regarding financial prosperity, it is absolutely God's will that we at least have enough for our needs, and even more. It's obviously not His will for us to create idols out of worldly possessions, but anyone whom the Lord has truly prospered knows that true riches are not in the world-they are in the spirit. While worldly riches certainly benefit us, they are temporary, should be submitted to the authority of the Lord, and managed with wisdom.

Salvation and the Infilling of the Holy Spirit

It is the desires of God that all men would be saved and experience eternal life. While not all experience this, it is nonetheless God's desire, and we should always take this position.

1 Timothy 2:3-4
This is good, and pleases God our Savior, who wants all people to be saved and to come to a knowledge of the truth.

He also desires that we be filled with the Spirit of God to be able to walk in power in the earth.

Acts 1:8

But you will receive power when the Holy Spirit comes on you; and you will be my witnesses in Jerusalem, and in all Judea and Samaria, and to the ends of the earth.

Luke 11:13

"If you then, though you are evil, know how to give good gifts to your children, how much more will your Father in heaven give the Holy Spirit to those who ask him!"

Wisdom & Direction

God doesn't want us to operate foolishly and blindly. He desires that we have wisdom and direction for our choices and actions, and He promises to provide it for us.

James 1:5 states that when we need wisdom, we need to seek it from the Lord and He will supply it generously. God can directly download wisdom into you, or He can get you the information you're looking for from other sources-reading your Bible, going to church, podcasts, YouTube videos, articles, books, people, etc.

Proverbs 3:5-6

Trust in the Lord with all your heart and lean not on your own understanding; in all your ways submit to him, and he will make your paths straight.

James 1:5
But if any of you lacks wisdom, let him ask of God, who gives to all generously and without reproach, and it will be given to him.

Turning Completely Away from Evil (Repentance)

Another aspect of God's will is that we turn completely away from evil. This may include renouncing things in our lives and going through deliverance to get completely free.

Often, people may ask you to intercede on their behalf, but do not want to make any necessary changes. It is God's will that we experience the entirety of His blessing as we turn from any sin in our lives and align with His Word.

Matthew 5: 3-4, emphasis mine
Blessed are the poor in spirit, for theirs is the kingdom of heaven. Blessed are those who mourn [for their sin], for they will be comforted.

2 Chronicles 7:14

If my people, who are called by my name, will humble themselves and pray and seek my face and turn from their wicked ways, then I will hear from heaven, and I will forgive their sin and I will heal their land.

Proverbs 3:7-8

Do not be wise in your own eyes; fear the Lord and shun evil. This will bring health to your body and nourishment to your bones.

Insight, Understanding, & Knowledge

Likewise, it's God's will that we operate from a place of knowledge and understanding, and He provides this for His children.

Proverbs 19:2

Desire without knowledge is not good-how much more will hasty feet miss the way!

Proverbs 4:5-7

Acquire wisdom! Acquire understanding! Do not forget nor turn away from the words of my mouth. Do not forsake her, and she will guard you; love her, and she will watch over you. The beginning of wisdom is: acquire wisdom, and with all your acquiring, get understanding.

Proverbs 2:6

For the Lord gives wisdom; from his mouth come knowledge and understanding.

Proverbs 18:15

The heart of the discerning acquires knowledge, for the ears of the wise seek it out.

Divine Intervention

There are situations that are beyond knowledge, wisdom, and even repentance-there are times where we literally need God to step in and move on our behalf. Supernatural intervention is the will of the Father. God has done it before, and He will do it again!

Exodus 14:21-22

Then Moses stretched out his hand over the sea; and the Lord swept the sea back by a strong east wind all night and turned the sea into dry land, so the waters were divided. The sons of Israel went through the midst of the sea on the dry land, and the waters were like a wall to them on their right hand and on their left.

Joshua 10:12-13

Then Joshua spoke to the Lord in the day when the Lord delivered up the Amorites before the sons of Israel, and he said in the sight of Israel,

"O sun, stand still at Gibeon, and O moon in the valley of Aijalon."
So the sun stood still, and the moon stopped, until the nation avenged themselves of their enemies. Is it not written in the book of Jashar? And the sun stopped in the middle of the sky and did not hasten to go down for about a whole day.

Justice

God does not overlook wrongdoing, especially when it's done to the innocent. He is the avenger of the widow, the orphan, and the poor, and of those who try to take advantage of such people will be met with the vengeance of the Lord.

However, it must be pointed out that all vengeance must be entrusted to God. We cannot be trusted with vengeance because we don't often have a heart of mercy.

Hebrews 10:30
For we know him who said, "It is mine to avenge; I will repay," and again, "the Lord will judge his people."

Hosea 12:6
But you must return to your God; maintain love and justice, and wait for your God always.

Romans 12:19

Do not take revenge, my dear friends, but leave room for God's wrath, for it is written: "It is mine to avenge; I will repay," says the Lord.

CHAPTER 2 QUESTIONS

1. Why is it important to settle in your heart what the will of God is in key areas?

2. How can we determine the revealed will of God toward humanity?

3. What is God's revealed will concerning healing?

4. What is God's revealed will concerning prosperity?

5. How should you pray if you aren't sure about what the will of God is concerning a situation?

CHAPTER 3

Intercession: What Exactly Is It?

We live in a day and age where there are false teachers everywhere. Churches are splitting because of issues ranging from the church's stance on politics to whether or not homosexuality is a sin. Likewise, Timothy also faced turmoil and false teachers during the early times of the church.

Paul the Apostle, who had planted the church Timothy was overseeing, heard about the false teachers Timothy was up against and wrote him a letter. In the letter, he addressed different things the false teachers were teaching and gave Timothy instructions on how to lead the church.

One of these instructions had to do with prayer. Paul told Timothy,

> "First of all, then, I urge that supplications, prayers, intercessions, and thanksgivings be made for all people, for kings and all who are in high positions, that we may lead a peaceful and quiet life, godly and dignified in every way. This is good, and it is

pleasing in the sight of God our Savior, who desires all people to be saved and to come to the knowledge of the truth. For there is one God, and there is one mediator between God and men, the man Christ Jesus, who gave himself as a ransom for all, which is the testimony given at the proper time" (1 Timothy 2:1-6 ESV).

Paul starts out the text by stating *first of all.* This means that what he's about to say at the beginning should have preeminence. Then, he *urges* Timothy. This is something worth paying attention to because when you urge someone, you're desperately trying to get them to do something important.

Paul was urging Timothy that prayer should have preeminence. But Paul does not simply just use the word prayer; he elaborates on the concept of prayer by breaking it down into four categories: supplications, prayers, intercession, and thanksgiving. Each of these types of prayers serve a purpose, so let's break each of them down.

Prayers of supplication are prayers in which an individual confidently and humbly, in a heartfelt manner, pleads with God for something. Jesus prayed prayers of supplication while here on earth. The Hebrew writer states this about Jesus' prayer life: "In the days of his flesh, Jesus offered up prayers and supplications, with loud cries and tears, to him who was able to save him from death, and he was heard because of his reverence" (Hebrews 5:7 ESV).

According to the writer of Hebrews, Jesus's prayer life was intense. He would cry out to God with tears of desperation, which means that the prayers He prayed were not silent but loud. This begs the question: should *our* prayer lives also be filled with such desperate cries to God? I'd say yes. We are to walk as Jesus walked (1 John 2:6 ESV).

After supplications, Paul talks about *prayers.* Regarding this, the Hebrew writer states that Jesus offered up prayers and supplications. By prayers, he may be indicating different types of prayers, or just a multitude of prayers. In Greek, the word for *pray* is *proseúxomai.* The word *proseúxomai* means to wish, or to exchange wishes. It carries the idea of *interacting with* the Lord by switching *human* wishes (ideas) for *His* wishes as He imparts faith (divine *persuasion*)[3].

So then, prayer is a divine exchange-you are taking ideas that may be corrupted by the flesh and exchanging them for God's wishes. The exchanging of wishes is not necessarily supplication, intercession, or thanksgiving[4]. Therefore, it should be categorized separately, just as Paul categorizes it.

Before we discuss intercession, let's talk about thanksgiving. In the Gospel of Luke, there is a story of Jesus sending out his disciples to minister to Israel. Upon their return, the disciples were filled with excitement because demons were cast out of people, in the name of Jesus, through them. While Jesus was delighted about their victory, He also cautioned them.

Jesus did not want the disciples to be only focused on the demonic world. It's dangerous for an individual to believe being heavenly minded is constantly thinking about the devil. Jesus made sure they understood that although demons leaving someone is good, this should not be the source of their joy. "Nevertheless, do not rejoice in this, that the spirits are subject to you, but rejoice that your names are written in heaven" (Luke 10:20 ESV).

Joy brought forth from what you do is fleeting and short-lived. True joy should flow from who you are in God. Therefore, the joy that a disciple of Jesus has should constantly come from the fact that he or she is a child of God.

While having a conversation with his disciples, Jesus broke out in thanksgiving to God. He "rejoiced in the Holy Spirit" and said:

> "I thank you, Father, Lord of heaven and earth, that you have hidden these things from the wise and understanding and revealed them to little children; yes, Father, for such was your gracious will. All things have been handed over to me by my Father, and no one knows who the Son is except the Father, or who the Father is except the Son and anyone to whom the Son chooses to reveal him" (Luke 10:21-22 ESV).

The thanksgiving Jesus gave to God the Father was in response to the Gospel conversation He had with the disciples. The Bible actually says *in that same hour.* In our translation, it could be at that very moment, right as he was speaking to them, that He started giving God thanks. This was not a supplication, nor was He asking God to do something. There was no intercession, He was not praying for someone, and there was no exchanging of wishes. He was just celebrating who God was and what God did.

This is exactly what prayers of thanksgiving are: prayers celebrating God for who He is and what He does. When you pray these prayers, joy will fill your heart. A mature believer comes to God first with a heart of thanksgiving, and he or she enters the courts of God's kingdom with praise (Psalm 100).

Lastly, there are prayers of intercession. Like all the other prayers, Jesus also prayed, and still prays, prayers of intercession.

During his final hours on earth, Jesus prayed:

> "'I do not ask for these only, but also for those who will believe in me through their word, that they may all be one, just as you, Father, are in me, and I in you, that they also may be in us, so that the world may believe that you have sent me. The glory that you have given me I have given to them, that they may be one even as we are one, I in them and you in me, that they may become perfectly one, so that the world may know that you sent me and loved them even as you loved me. Father, I desire that they also, whom you have given me, may be with me where I am, to see my glory that you have given me because you loved me before the foundation of the world. O righteous Father, even though the world does not know you, I know you, and these know that you have sent me. I made known to them your name, and I will continue to make it known, that the love with which you have loved me may be in them, and I in them'" (John 17:20-26 ESV).

Right before Jesus was about to be crucified, He was interceding for others. This is a good lesson for us- when we are going through something difficult, we must still make time to pray for others. Jesus interceded for those who God had placed under His care and those, in the future, who would one day respond to the Gospel (John 17:20).

You and I are in the family of God because Jesus prayed for us 2,000 years ago. Prayers of intercession can change generations. It's time for the intercessors to arise!

The anchor of all these four prayers has got to be God. It's His heart that one should be persuaded to reflect. As Paul writes, "This is good, and it is pleasing in the sight of God our Savior, who desires all people to be saved and to come to the knowledge of the truth" (1 Timothy 2:3-4 ESV).

The desire for prayer is not innate to us, but it can be grown in us as we intimately spend time with Jesus. God is the one who desires all people to be saved, so prayer accomplishes His desire for restoration-not ours. Therefore, as our hearts grow to mirror God's heart, we will desire to pray with the right motives.

CHAPTER 3 QUESTIONS

1. What was the primary thing Paul urged Timothy to do pertaining to how he should lead the church?

2. What is supplication and in what situation would you use it?

3. Prayer is a _____ _____-you are taking ideas that may be corrupted by the flesh and exchanging them for God's wishes.

4. A believer should come to God first with prayers of
    _____.

5. What should be our response when we are going through something difficult?

CHAPTER 4

Seven Qualities of an Intercessor

There are seven characteristics that show that someone is an intercessor or has the potential to become an intercessor. These seven characteristics are love, forgiveness, passion, compassion, discernment, knowledge, and prayerfulness. When an individual displays these characteristics, it is easy to know that they either have the potential to become an intercessor or that they are an intercessor.

The first important characteristic is love. The Bible says,

> "If anyone says, "I love God," and hates his brother, he is a liar; for he who does not love his brother whom he has seen cannot love God whom he has not seen. And this commandment we have from him: whoever loves God must also love his brother" (1 John 4:20-21 ESV).

Loving God and loving others are synonymous, and a person cannot truly intercede for others unless they understand this.

It's important to understand that this kind of love that John speaks about is not natural. The word love here in the Greek is *agapé* and it means "unconditional love". No man can love another man unconditionally without the help of the Holy Spirit.

Keeping this in mind, one must understand that this type of love is imparted in our hearts from the Holy Spirit as we seek Him. Our job, therefore, is to admit we don't have this love and be willing to ask for it from God.

The next quality that helps define an intercessor is forgiveness. As we just read in 1 John, one cannot hate his brother or sister and say they love God. An unforgiving heart is a heart susceptible to hate.

If there was anyone who had the right to not forgive it would have been Jesus. But on the cross, He chose to release us by saying, "…Father, forgive them, for they know not what they do…" (Luke 23:34 ESV). As He was bleeding on the cross, He was interceding for all of us!

This is the example Christians must follow. Biblically speaking forgiveness is not an optional thing. Jesus puts it like this, "…if you forgive others their trespasses, your heavenly Father will also forgive you, but if you do not forgive others their trespasses, neither will your Father forgive your trespasses" (Matthew 6:14-15 ESV).

Next, an intercessor must be passionate. In the Scriptures we read this about passion, "Never be lacking in zeal, but keep your spiritual fervor, serving the Lord" (Romans 12:11). The word *zeal* and *fervor* are synonymous with the word passion. Paul in this text is saying as we work for the Lord, we should be enthusiastic about our service.

Passion persuades action. It's difficult for someone who burns with zeal to not be real. Intercessors must be action prone and genuine about their spiritual walk with the Lord.

Following passion an intercessor should have compassion. Compassion can at times be mistaken with love. However, love is a deep feeling of affection and connection towards an individual, whereas compassion is a sympathetic pity that causes you to be concerned for the sufferings or misfortunes of others[5]. Compassion is not just thinking about someone's misfortunes; it is a deep concern that comes from the inner part of you[6].

Jesus was moved on many occasions by compassion (Isaiah 40:11; Isaiah 42:3; Isaiah 63:9; Luke 7:13; Matthew

11:28-30; Matthew 14:14; Hebrews 2:17). One of the shortest verses in Scripture is John 11:35 and it simply says, "Jesus wept." In context, Jesus was weeping after His friend Lazarus had passed away.

Jesus did not weep because Lazarus died, but because He had deep pity and sympathy for humanity. As He saw Martha and Mary weeping it touched His heart. Right after this moment Jesus prayed to His Father, called Lazarus out of the tomb, and Lazarus resurrected (John 11:35-44).

Like Jesus, each intercessor should be filled with compassion. The way to acquire this type of compassion, according to Scripture, is to put it on by faith. In Colossians 3:12, the Bible says to clothe ourselves "with compassion, kindness, humility, gentleness and patience."

Furthermore, intercessors also should be equipped with discernment. The Hebrew writer says this about discernment,

> "For though by this time you ought to be teachers, you need someone to teach you again the basic principles of the oracles of God. You need milk, not solid food, for everyone who lives on milk is unskilled in the word of righteousness, since he is a child. But solid food is for the mature, for those who have their powers of discernment trained by

constant practice to distinguish good from evil" (Hebrews 5:12-14 ESV).

The writer of Hebrews is gently rebuking the believers he is admonishing. He is explaining to them that Christians must grow and mature, and that part of this maturity includes the ability to discern.

Discernment is formed as you constantly practice how to distinguish between good and evil. This discernment is different from the gift of discerning of spirits, which is a gift from the Holy Spirit that does not require maturity. Those who are used in the gift of discerning of spirits still must grow in it, but it will be easier for them to flow in this gifting as it is gifted to them by the Holy Spirit.

Now the training and practicing takes place as we are participating in the things of God, such as reading our Bibles, witnessing, praying, fellowshipping with other believers, and listening to sound doctrine. A mature intercessor will have their powers of discernment trained, and they will be able to distinguish between right and wrong.

Alongside discernment, it is important for every intercessor to have knowledge. The Bible says that God's people are destroyed from lack of knowledge, and that because they have rejected knowledge, God will also reject them as His priests, "…because you have ignored the law of your God, I also will ignore your children" (Hosea 4:6). God was speaking through Hosea the prophet in this passage and is rebuking the Israelites who have committed apostasy.

God says because they had rejected knowledge, He also rejected them as priests. One of the jobs of the priest was to intercede on the behalf of the people of Israel. Therefore, their rejection of knowledge stripped them of their ability to intercede and distanced them from God.

Now the word knowledge here in Hebrew is the word *daath*, and it means knowledge of God and it is connected to obedience[7]. Peter also used this word when he spoke about the eight virtues that all believers should possess if they want to be fruitful (2 Peter 1:5-7). Daath does not refer to book knowledge, but rather theological heartfelt knowledge that seeks to understand who God is.

If an intercessor rejects this knowledge, they will be ineffective in the kingdom of God. Intercessors must know the heart of God, and to know the heart of God, one must truly study God. Not to gain head knowledge, but to understand who God is.

Last but not least, all intercessors or those aspiring to be intercessors must be prayerful. By prayerful I don't mean they must spend countless time praying, but rather that they should desire to spend quality time with God. It could be five minutes or seven hours -that must be determined by the beckoning of the Spirit.

For Solomon says,

> "Guard your steps when you go to the house of God. Go near to listen rather than to offer the sacrifice of fools, who do not know that they do wrong. Do not be quick with your mouth, do not be hasty in your heart to utter anything before God. God is in heaven and you are on earth, so let your words be few" (Ecclesiastes 5:1-2 NIV).

Indeed, Jesus prayed at times throughout the night and we will at times probably be led to do likewise. However, our relationship with God should not be dictated by how many words we speak to Him.

Sometimes it's in silence that we show our reliance on God. There are times when we will have to be still and know that God is God and that He will be exalted (Psalm 46:10). Should we long to spend more time with God? Yes! But does spending long times in prayer mean we know God? Not necessarily. This is why it's important for intercessors to *really seek to know God.*

CHAPTER 4 QUESTIONS

1. A person cannot truly intercede for others unless they understand what?

2. No man can love another unconditionally without what?

3. What's the difference between love and compassion? How do you acquire compassion?

4. According to the author, how do we develop discernment?

5. How is knowledge connected to obedience?

CHAPTER 5

The Beginning of My Intercessory Journey

In February of 1993, after giving my life to Christ, I found myself in a huge mental and spiritual battle. I was thinking about my dad and the challenging relationship I had with him, and how the spirits in my life that had come in through a voodoo priest wanted to grab me back. There were also friends of mine who had no interest in being my friends. Needless to say, I was in a tough place mentally, emotionally, and spiritually.

I visited a church with my friend Alex. While the church was nice, I felt like that church wasn't able to help me the way I needed. Because of that, I told Alex that I needed to find a church that could help me fight the battle that I was facing, so my other friend, Gerald, took me to a different church on a Wednesday morning. As soon as I got there, I felt the presence of God and I had an urge to pray. We spent time there praying, and that was when my prayer life was born.

When I went back home, I started reading the book of Acts, and while reading, I had a vision. On a clear day, I saw someone with a long robe who stood before me. He said to me, "I need you to go do just like the apostles." He repeatedly called my name, Ansy. However, I was so scared because I never had a vision like this.

But someone told me that it was God that was speaking to me and it had to do with my calling. Following this experience, I spoke with my friends concerning our prayer lives. I felt like we needed to start interceding for our town. The desire for intercession began to arise in me, and the more time I spent interceding, the more my hunger for intercession grew.

During this time of my life, I helped lead many young men and women to Christ. Some of them I led personally, and some came to church with me and gave their lives to Christ there. Through our intercession, a huge spiritual movement began that later gave birth to many spiritual warriors.

There was a warlock named Morris who used to have a voodoo ceremony twice a year in our neighborhood. People came from everywhere to attend the ceremony. But one day I called Alex and Gerald and said to them, "If we pray, we could stop this voodoo ritual in this town."

They agreed with me. Alex's house was next door to the voodoo priest's house, so Gerald and I got to his house early in the morning, prior to the voodoo dance, after having fasted all day.

The voodoo ceremony started in the morning with Satanic worship and other sacrificial rituals. We prayed prayers of intercession and the presence of the Holy Spirit fell in Alex's house. We asked God to stop every demonic spirit trafficking in the area in the name of Jesus.

It worked! The entire ceremony halted because the spirits that they were attempting to conjure were never able to manifest. The voodoo priest was so mad that he came in front of Alex's house and started screaming my name. "Ansy, come outside because you are stopping me from doing my ritual."

He repeated himself a second time. The people were afraid for me to come out. He had a machete in his hand and a purple handkerchief around his neck.

I opened the door. I respectfully asked him if he was okay. He said, "You stopped my ceremony."

"I didn't do anything against you," I responded. "What makes you say that?"

He replied, "You were praying to your Jesus and made everything stop." Right then, I began to have more confidence in intercession because I realized that my prayers had actually stopped a voodoo ceremony. He then put a rock on a fire, and people thought He was doing something spiritual to put a curse on me.

Because the voodoo priest was not able to summon the evil spirits, the ceremony wasn't able to take place, and everyone left. The next morning, the voodoo priest came to me and said, "I see the power that is in you guys, but you guys have to stop bothering me."

I said, "We were just simply praying. We weren't bothering you at all."

"I do this not because I know it isn't good, but this is how I provide for my family," he replied.

"God could give you directions to supply for your family the right way," I stated.

Then he said, "One day I will join you guys." Unfortunately, he passed away without giving his life to Christ. His children, on the other hand, gave their lives to Christ and they refused to serve those evil spirits. They also burned every voodoo artifact.

One day, when I was living in America, his daughter called me and said,

"Ansy, I gave my life to Christ. I even threw away everything my dad was doing. Because I knew that day that you were praying that the power of God stopped everything that my father was doing. I was very confused, because I thought that my dad was a very powerful man until that day. That's why I made up my mind to make a total transition from the dark world to embrace Jesus Christ as my personal savior. The way God used you that day will remain forever in my mind. I didn't have the power to tell my dad what I was thinking concerning the voodoo ritual that we used to do twice a year. But I knew I had no belief in him doing those things anymore. That's the reason I gave my life to Christ. Thank you so much, for allowing God to use you, so that my eyes could be opened this much to turn away from the dark world."

After hearing her testimony, I felt so great inside. I never even knew until she shared the testimony how much God had used our intercession to save her life. She wasn't the only one God delivered during those years either, for our intercession birthed an awakening. People started respecting us so much, and we started a prayer meeting once a month from 6 am to 6 pm. Everyone started coming to me to help solve their issues, including seeking for healing. This ended up turning into an annual crusade that lasted 6-7 years.

People began praying like never before, and they started to intercede for one another. As a result, we started seeing signs and wonders for the first time. A revival exploded and people were calling me left and right to preach, pray for the sick, and to cast out demonic spirits from people.

CHAPTER 5 QUESTIONS

1. Through his encounter with the voodoo priest, what did the author realize about the power of intercession?

2. Prayer has the power to make things happen in the earth. Discuss a time when you witnessed things happen in your life or in someone else's life as a response to your prayers.

CHAPTER 6

Intercession Testimony: Freed from Prison!

Intercession can bring people out of prison. In the book of Acts, we read about how Peter was imprisoned by King Herod. This imprisonment was not a temporary one, for King Herod was going to behead Peter to please the people.

But the Bible says,

"So Peter was kept in prison, but the church was earnestly praying to God for him. The night before Herod was to bring him to trial, Peter was sleeping between two soldiers, bound with two chains, and sentries stood guard at the entrance. Suddenly an angel of the Lord appeared, and a light shone in the cell. He struck Peter on the side and woke him up. "Quick, get up!" he said, and the chains fell off Peter's wrists. Then the angel said to him, "Put on your clothes and sandals." And Peter did so. "Wrap your cloak around you and follow me," the angel told him. Peter followed him out of the prison, but he had no idea that what the angel was doing was really happening; he thought he was seeing a vision. They passed the first and second guards and came to the iron gate leading to the city. It opened for them by itself, and they went through it. When they had walked the length of one street, suddenly the angel left him. Then Peter came to himself and said, "Now I know without a doubt that the Lord has sent his angel and rescued me from Herod's clutches and from everything the Jewish people were hoping would happen" (Acts 12:5-11).

In response to Peter's imprisonment, the church prayed passionately, zealously, and fervently, burning in anguish for him to be released. They didn't just say a simple prayer-they interceded intentionally and purposefully. The text doesn't say that only a few people were interceding, but that the *church* did, meaning it was a united front.

As they prayed earnestly, God heard them and sent an angel to take Peter out of prison. After the angel struck Peter on the side and told him to get up, his chains fell off his wrists. The church's intercession opened the prison door for Peter. An angel woke him up, unchained him, clothed him, walked him past the guards, opened the prison gate, helped walk him to freedom, and saved him from death.

This is what I call deliverance! Intercession and deliverance go hand and hand. Many people are imprisoned like Peter by an evil king: the devil.

Only through your prayers will they be set free. Before Peter was locked up, the Scripture says that James was imprisoned by King Herod and beheaded. It's interesting that there is no mention of the church praying in the same way for James as they did for Peter.

Maybe the church was distracted by their own trials. Maybe the fact that they were being persecuted so heavily made them more focused on themselves. Whatever the reason may have been, we do not read of them crying out to God for James.

You can't help but wonder if something different could have happened if the church prayed like they prayed for Peter. Likewise, when we don't intercede for those who are spiritually in bondage, death is what may await them as well.

This type of intercessory prayer that gets people out of spiritual prison is different from the others. It takes intentionality, and your mind must be ready for war. God has called us to deliver people out of spiritual prisons just like Peter was delivered out of a physical prison.

For us to accomplish this, we must understand what deliverance is. The church for too long has just let the evil king, Satan, imprison people and eventually kill them. We must engage in the battle like the church did for Peter!

God's Deliverance for My Spiritual Daughter

One of my spiritual daughters broke the law when she was very young. She committed a crime at her workplace. She deserved to be sentenced to jail but was let go.

Years after she committed this crime, she received a letter in the mail. To her disbelief, the letter was from Pennsylvania's high court. The letter stated that she had to be retried by the State of Pennsylvania's Department of Justice.

Hearing that she would be retried was very painful news for her. Her heart completely dropped because at this point, she had changed and made a whole new transformation in her life. I received a call from her that night and she sounded very sad, so I asked her what was wrong.

She explained to me everything about the previous trials and that the case was closed unprejudiced, meaning other judges could just decide to retry the case if they chose to. We contacted a lawyer to represent my spiritual daughter. On the day of her trial, her brother and I went in and sat in anticipation of the verdict.

The prosecutor brought many convincing pieces of evidence in hopes the judge would rule against my spiritual daughter. I believed that our lawyer presented just as much evidence and argued the case very well. However, the judge ruled against my spiritual daughter.

He sentenced her to five years in prison and deportation afterwards. I was so upset that tears just started to flow. The lawyer said to me, "Sir, this is my card. She can give me a call from the jail cell," and he left.

I remember saying, "Lord! You didn't tell me that she was going to stay behind." As I sat there, people were saying I did not understand how the justice system works in America because I didn't believe she was supposed to be in jail. I went outside the courtroom, sat down, and began to intercede for her.

I told God, "I'm not leaving this place without my spiritual daughter." I couldn't raise my voice because some of the courtrooms were still in session. I sat in the lobby interceding for two hours straight.

At one point someone told me that I should leave the place because the trial was over. Suddenly, at 3 pm an officer from the court came out and asked me, "Are you Pastor Ansy, the Pastor of the lady that was incarcerated?"

"Yes," I responded.

The officer continued, "This is the first time in the history of the United States of America's justice system that a judge is making such a decision against a ruling. She is being freed from custody and she will be going home with you."

I was shocked! I didn't know how to thank God for hearing and responding to my intercession. This reminded me of when Peter got set free and the young lady who came to the door when Peter was knocking, saw it was Peter and was so delighted that she forgot to open the door (Acts 12:13). I was rendered speechless by the greatness of my God who could even take prisoners out of prison!

CHAPTER 6 QUESTIONS

1. In response to imprisonment, how did the church pray? What happened as a result?

2. According to the author, what does it take to pray prayers that get people out of spiritual prison?

3. In response to his intercession, what did the author see happen to his spiritual daughter?

CHAPTER 7

Interceding for Those Who Have Wronged You

My dad and I never had a good relationship. I was rejected by him when my mother was pregnant with me. He did not want me to be born, so he tried to force my mom to abort me.

The abortion attempt failed, so my mom decided to keep me. My dad was not happy, so he lashed out at her and made her leave. When she left Haiti for America, she couldn't take me with her, so I was left behind with my dad.

As a young man, he never acknowledged me as his son. He would call me names like "animal", but he would never call me "son" and he did not want me to call him "Dad". That brought so much confusion to my life, and the pain of it made me feel as if my heart was bleeding.

Growing up with this kind of hurt in my heart caused me to make bad choices with my life. But when I gave my life to Christ, I traveled to America to join my mother before going to Boston to see my dad.

I started interceding for my dad even when my heart was bleeding from the abuse I'd received from him. I knew I had unforgiveness in my heart, so I prayed that God would help me forgive. God, who mends the broken-hearted (Luke 4:18), mended my bleeding heart as I interceded for my dad and gave me the strength to forgive him.

I went to Boston and I gave my dad a hug and spent time with him. Through the power of the Holy Spirit, I showed him love despite how he treated me. As a result, he gave his life to Christ the same week that he was going to die.

Before he passed away, we were able to reconcile and build a great relationship. My dad, who spoke nothing but evil to me while I was growing up, was the first one to call me Pastor.

I thank God for the power of intercession! What if I had decided to not intercede for him? What if I had allowed revenge to drive me instead of love? My dad would never have come to Jesus! Through intercession, my heart changed, and God moved. One day I will see my dad in heaven!

Brothers and sisters, we as believers should not die with grudges. The Bible states, "But if you do not forgive others their sins, your Father will not forgive your sins" (Matthew 6:15).

We must release those who have harmed us. One cannot fully intercede for others if one refuses to release offense. Imagine what would have happened if Abraham chose to be offended with his nephew Lot for leaving him! His nephew Lot even took the greener pastures when he left. But Abraham did not allow offense to stop him from loving his nephew Lot, and even went to war for him (Genesis 13:5-13).

Would you go to war for someone who abandoned you? Or would you say that they deserved the calamity because of how they treated you? Even after going to war on his behalf, Abraham didn't put any expectations on Lot.

He did not say "Lot, you owe me because I delivered you." When you intercede, you are going to war for someone like Abraham went to war for Lot. You don't do it for a reward, but to set the person free!

CHAPTER 7 QUESTIONS

1. What happened as a result of the author interceding for his dad?

2. We should not die with _____.

3. According to the author, we cannot fully intercede for someone if we carry offense. Why do you think this is?

4. Think of someone who has recently done something offensive to you. What has been your response to this person? Did you intercede for him or her? If not, take a few moments now to release them and intercede for them.

CHAPTER 8

Why Some Prayers Are Not Answered

Have you ever wondered why some of your prayers of intercession were not answered? Some people refuse to pray because maybe they prayed for something or someone in the past and nothing happened. In their hearts, they may believe that God has not answered their prayers.

Let's look at the different possible reasons why God may not answer someone's prayers. The prophet Samuel was an amazing intercessor, yet not everything he prayed for was answered the way he may have thought it should have been.

After King Saul disobeyed God, God rejected him from being King. Samuel, being the intercessor he was, mourned for Saul. The Lord spoke to him and said,

> "How long will you mourn for Saul, since I have rejected him as king over Israel? Fill your horn with oil and be on your way; I am sending you to Jesse

of Bethlehem. I have chosen one of his sons to be king" (1 Samuel 16:1).

Did God tell Samuel to stop interceding for Saul's soul? No. God's statement had to do with Saul being king over Israel.

God did not reject Saul as a person-Saul rejected God as king over his life, so God rejected his kingship. Intercession is not about getting people in the right position, but about people's hearts being positioned in the right place. The Bible says,

> "What causes fights and quarrels among you? Don't they come from your desires that battle within you? You desire but do not have, so you kill. You covet but you cannot get what you want, so you quarrel and fight. You do not have because you do not ask God. When you ask, you do not receive, because you ask with wrong motives, that you may spend what you get on your pleasures" (James 4:1-3).

Again, a person's motives matter. The *why* you are praying is more important than the *how* you are praying.

With this in mind, there are a few reasons why a person's prayers may not be answered. Firstly, James says that we have not because we ask not. Some people never ask, so they never receive.

Following this, James talks about wrong desires. This doesn't only cover sinful desires, but seemingly good desires that may not line up with the will of God. This can be seen, for instance, when Samuel prayed for Saul to be repositioned as king.

Another reason an individual's prayers may not be answered is because they're in disunity with their spouse. Peter says,

> "In the same way, you husbands must give honor to your wives. Treat your wife with understanding as you live together. She may be weaker than you are, but she is your equal partner in God's gift of new life. Treat her as you should so your prayers will not be hindered" (1 Peter 3:7 NLT).

Next, if there is disunity in the marriage, your prayers may not be answered. Furthermore, even your children may experience ungodliness due to disunity in marriage. In the book of Malachi, God says this about marriage:

> "Here is another thing you do. You cover the Lord's altar with tears, weeping and groaning because he pays no attention to your offerings and doesn't accept them with pleasure. You cry out, 'Why doesn't the Lord accept my worship?' I'll tell you why! Because the Lord witnessed the vows you and your wife made when you were young. But you have been unfaithful to her, though she remained

your faithful partner, the wife of your marriage vows. Didn't the Lord make you one with your wife? In body and spirit you are his. And what does he want? Godly children from your union. So guard your heart; remain loyal to the wife of your youth. 'For I hate divorce!' says the Lord, the God of Israel. 'To divorce your wife is to overwhelm her with cruelty,' says the Lord of Heaven's Armies. 'So guard your heart; do not be unfaithful to your wife'" (Malachi 2:13-16 NLT).

God makes it very clear that what he desires for marriage is unity (oneness). God says through unity in marriage is birthed godly offspring. Without unity, we can cry till we're blue in the face and certain prayers we pray may still not be answered.

This is one thing Samuel may have neglected, and it birthed in part a desire for something worldly in the people he was leading. Samuel's kids were wicked, and the people were fearful of them taking charge after Samuel died.

"As Samuel grew old, he appointed his sons to be judges over Israel. Joel and Abijah, his oldest sons, held court in Beersheba. But they were not like their father, for they were greedy for money. They accepted bribes and perverted justice. Finally, all the elders of Israel met at Ramah to discuss the matter with Samuel. "Look," they told him, "you are now old, and your sons are not like you. Give us a king to judge us like all the other nations have" (1 Samuel 8:1-5 NLT).

Our first ministry must be to our family. If we're not diligent in this, all the work we put in may die with us. Are you neglecting your wife? Are you neglecting your children? If so, repent today!

The first place a person should be an intercessor is in their home. Cry out for your marriage first. Pray with your own household first. If they know the Lord or are willing to know Him, pray with them.

Another thing that can halt a person's prayers is gossiping. Sometimes, intercession meetings turn into gossip sessions. You should not bless and curse out of the same mouth (James 3).

Gossip is rooted in selfish ambition and jealousy. The Bible says that jealousy and selfishness are not God's kind of wisdom. These things are "...earthly, unspiritual, and demonic. For wherever there is jealousy and selfish ambition, there you will find disorder and evil of every kind" (James 3:15-16 NLT). One cannot intercede with this kind of heart.

Also, a person's intercession can be impeded by a critical spirit. In the Old Testament there is a story of King David dancing with all his might as he ushered in the presence of God. While he danced, his wife became critical of him, and she despised him in her heart (2 Samuel 6:12-16).

When David made it home his wife Michal stated, "How the king of Israel has distinguished himself today, going around half-naked in full view of the slave girls of his servants as any vulgar fellow would!" (2 Samuel 6:20). David responded by saying, "'I will become even more undignified than this, and I will be humiliated in my own eyes. But by these slave girls you spoke of, I will be held in honor'" (2 Samuel 6:22). David was more concerned with God receiving glory than what men thought of him, even if it meant he looked foolish.

The last verse of this chapter is one that people must not forget. The verse says that "Michal daughter of Saul had no children to the day of her death" (2 Samuel 6:23). A critical spirit can cause you to be barren.

This means when you choose to criticize others instead of encouraging others, you will see things blocked in your life. Dreams that you may have had will not come to pass, missed opportunities will become common, doors that could have been opened shall remain shut, and your intercession cannot be effective. Nothing is birthed where a critical spirit is.

The last thing that can hinder intercession is not truly knowing the Lord. "The Lord is far from the wicked, but he hears the prayers of the righteous" (Proverbs 15:29 NLT). When someone doesn't know the Lord, they should not expect all their prayers to be answered.

CHAPTER 8 QUESTIONS

1. Intercession is not about getting people in the right position, but about people's hearts being _____ in the right place.

2. The _____ you are praying matters more than the _____ you are praying.

3. According to the book of James, we can have _____ desires that don't line up with the _____ _____ _____ _____.

4. Our first ministry must be to whom? Where is the first place you must be an intercessor?

5. According to the author, what can you see happen in your life if you choose to operate in a critical spirit?

CHAPTER 9

Biblical Intercessors: Abraham

Now that we've looked at what intercession is, let's look at people in the Bible whom God molded into intercessors and learn from their lives.

There are times when destruction comes because no one is interceding. In Genesis 18, we read a story about Abraham negotiating with God for Sodom and Gomorrah in hopes to save his nephew Lot. Abraham pleaded with God to save the city if He could find even ten righteous people there.

This passage shows the importance of an intercessor to the world. Abraham stood in the gap, but without his prayers, who knows if Lot and his family would have been spared? When Lot delayed in leaving Sodom and Gomorrah, we read,

"With the coming of dawn, the angels urged Lot, saying, "Hurry! Take your wife and your two daughters who are here, or you will be swept away when the city is punished." When he hesitated, the men grasped his hand and the hands of his wife and of his two daughters and led them safely out of the city, for the Lord was merciful to them" (Genesis 19:15-16).

This is the only time in Scripture an angel physically grabbed people by the hand and led them to safety! One person's intercession can override another person's will. God does not desire to force man to do anything, but the force behind intercession can accomplish many things. During intercession, God's mercy shelters many from His wrath.

Even though Abraham asked God if He would spare His wrath if He could find only ten righteous people, the Bible clearly states that God would spare a whole city for the sake of one person. "I looked for someone among them who would build up the wall and stand before me in the gap on behalf of the land so I would not have to destroy it, but I found no one" (Ezekiel 22:30). Likewise, we read in Jeremiah that if God found one person who sought truth, He would spare the whole city.

> "Go up and down the streets of Jerusalem, look around and consider, search through her squares. If you can find but one person who deals honestly and

seeks the truth, I will forgive this city" (Jeremiah 5:1).

Abraham could have asked God to save Sodom and Gomorrah for the sake of one righteous person! God does not want to destroy people; He does not rejoice in harming us (Lamentation 3:33). Peter states, "the Lord is not slow in keeping his promise, as some understand slowness. Instead, He is patient with you, not wanting anyone to perish, but everyone to come to repentance" (2 Peter 3:9).

Do you know what else is interesting about this story? God was going to spare Sodom and Gomorrah if they chose to be hospitable and did not act despicably towards the angels, Lot, and his family. For God told Abraham "I am going down to see if their actions are as wicked as I have heard. If not, I want to know" (Genesis 18:21 NLT).

God was not coming down with the intention of harming Sodom and Gomorrah but in hopes the outcry was not true, he was giving them one final trial[8]. Lot, being the righteous man he was, showed hospitality to the angels without knowing they were angels. If the people of the city would have let them be, I believe the city would not have been judged (Genesis 19:3-13).

God's heart is that everyone would come to repentance and that none would perish. We've already established that in God's heart, mercy triumphs over judgment, and to intercede is to know this and extend this mercy toward others.

If God is so full of mercies, then why must we intercede? We must intercede because dominion over the earth was given to humanity according to God's words (Genesis 1:28). Therefore, God will not violate His word by moving without us allowing Him to. Even God's justice occurs on behalf of the outcries of the innocent.

Did you know that Lot also negotiated for a city and God spared the whole city? The angels wanted Lot to flee to the mountains because they were going to destroy even the cities nearby Sodom and Gomorrah as well. Yet Lot pleaded with the angels and the city was spared.

> "But Lot said to them, "No, my Lords, please! Your servant has found favor in your eyes, and you have shown great kindness to me in sparing my life. But I can't flee to the mountains; this disaster will overtake me, and I'll die. Look, here is a town near enough to run to, and it is small. Let me flee to it— it is very small, isn't it? Then my life will be spared." He said to him, "Very well, I will grant this request too; I will not overthrow the town you speak of. But flee there quickly, because I cannot do

anything until you reach it." (That is why the town was called Zoar.) By the time Lot reached Zoar, the sun had risen over the land" (Genesis 19:18-23).

Clearly the angels were going to destroy this city as well, but because Lot pleaded with them, they spared it. If God is willing to spare a small and insignificant place like Zoar, that was previously named Bela (meaning "destruction"), do you think your town or city is too far gone?[9]

CHAPTER 9 QUESTIONS

1. In this chapter, we read about how God would spare a whole city on account of even one righteous person. What does this reveal about the heart of God?

2. God does not want to _____ people; He does not rejoice in _____ us.

3. God's heart is that everyone would come to
_____.

4. Why must we intercede if God is full of mercy?

CHAPTER 10

Biblical Intercessors: Moses

Another great intercessor in the Old Testament was Moses. In Psalms, David wrote:

"At Horeb they made a calf and worshiped an idol cast from metal. They exchanged their glorious God for an image of a bull, which eats grass. They forgot the God who saved them, who had done great things in Egypt, miracles in the land of Ham and awesome deeds by the Red Sea. So he said he would destroy them— had not Moses, his chosen one, stood in the breach before him to keep his wrath from destroying them" (Psalms 106:19-23).

According to David, if Moses had not stood in the breach (gap), then God's wrath would have destroyed the children of Israel because of their idolatry. God told Moses, "Now leave me alone so that my anger may burn against them and that I may destroy them. Then I will make you into a great nation" (Exodus 32:10). What an offer!

Many of us today would have said, "Ok God," and would have helped God hit the restart button. God was ready to make a great nation out of Moses-all he had to do was agree with God to destroy them.

Moses, however, was not focused on how great he was going to be but on what was going to happen to God's great name.

> "But Moses sought the favor of the Lord his God. "Lord," he said, "why should your anger burn against your people, whom you brought out of Egypt with great power and a mighty hand? Why should the Egyptians say, 'It was with evil intent that he brought them out, to kill them in the mountains and to wipe them off the face of the earth'? Turn from your fierce anger; relent and do not bring disaster on your people. Remember your servants Abraham, Isaac and Israel, to whom you swore by your own self: 'I will make your descendants as numerous as the stars in the sky and I will give your descendants all this land I promised them, and it will be their inheritance forever.'" Then the Lord relented and did not bring on his people the disaster he had threatened" (Exodus 32:11-14).

Notice how Moses responded to God when God said he was going to make him a great nation and destroy the children of Israel. Moses pleaded for God to have mercy for His namesake. Moses believed that if God destroyed the children of Israel, the Egyptians would think evil of God.

God's reputation, therefore, was the reason Moses interceded. Moses cared more about God's name being glorified than the fact that people weren't living righteous. He reminded God of His promises to Abraham, Isaac, and Jacob.

He reiterates to God His own words that He had declared to the patriarchs. For God told the forefathers of Israel, "'...I will make your descendants as numerous as the stars in the sky and I will give your descendants all this land I promised them, and it will be their inheritance forever'" (Exodus 32:13). Similarly, we too must intercede, not only because it is our duty, but because Jesus Christ died for the world.

What would people say about our Lord if he destroyed the land we lived in? How would people view the cross that He was slain on? Oh Lord, for your namesake, relent and have mercy on our nations!

There are three important things we should glean from Moses' intercession. The first thing is that your motivation matters. If Moses was praying to receive a reward, then he would have told God to simply destroy the children of Israel. When we intercede, we must be motivated by the love of God and people.

Secondly, God's mercy reveals to the world His love. Moses believed that if God destroyed the children of Israel, then people would think God had evil intentions. Moses did not want people thinking this way about God. Are you okay with people thinking this way about God today?

Lastly, Moses used Gods' own words. He reminded God of His promises (Exodus 32:13). There is no greater tool when it comes to interceding than declaring to God His own words.

CHAPTER 10 QUESTIONS

1. If Moses had not interceded, God would have destroyed the nation of Israel. Why?

2. What was Moses concerned would happen if God destroyed Israel?

3. Has there ever been a time where you interceded with the wrong motives? Explain.

4. According to the author, what does God's mercy reveal to the world?

5. Moses did not want to believe that God had evil intentions toward humanity. Have you ever thought about how your representation of God affects how people around you see Him? Explain.

CHAPTER 11

Biblical Intercessors: Samuel

The next great intercessor in the Old Testament we can learn from is the prophet, Samuel. Samuel, whose name means "God hears", was an answer to prayer himself. Samuel's mom, Hannah, was barren and she pleaded with God for a child.

She told God that if He granted her request for a child, she would give that child to the Lord to serve the Lord his whole life. God heard her prayers and gave her a child she named Samuel. After Samuel was born, Hannah nursed him and then brought him to the house of God and placed him in the care of Eli the priest (1 Samuel 1:10-28).

Samuel stayed in the house of God, near the presence of God, and submitted to the man of God. In turn, God spoke to him. If one wants to provoke the voice of God, one must do the three things Samuel did. They are vital for every intercessor, and any intercessor who doesn't adhere to them is just shooting at the wind. Their prayers will not cause any damage to the kingdom of darkness because they refuse to commit to God's process.

God called Samuel three times and Samuel could not discern God's voice because he did not know the Lord yet, and God's Word had not yet been revealed to him (1 Samuel 3:7). It wasn't that he never read the Word of God, but rather that Samuel had yet to get a revelation of who God was.

Without revelation, there will be no manifestation, and without manifestation, there will be no demonstration. Samuel was in the house of God and in the very presence of God and yet he didn't know the Lord.

With God, there will always be more to adore-there is no ceiling to a God who keeps revealing. This is why we must press into God. There comes a time where the faith you have becomes your own faith and not the faith of those around you. Samuel, until this point, had yet to truly know God for himself.

Each time God called Samuel, Samuel thought it was Eli. It was only after the third time that Eli the Priest realized that it was God who had been speaking to the boy. Following this realization, Eli taught Samuel how to respond to God's calling.

Although God called Samuel, God didn't do anything but call Samuel's name until Samuel responded. And Samuel didn't respond until he was taught how to do so by the person he was submitting to. *God may call us, but it is our job to respond.*

Our response is made easier when we're in the house of God, in the presence of God, and submitting to the man or woman of God. Samuel did not submit to a perfect man either, for God told Samuel this about Eli,

> "Then the Lord said to Samuel, "Behold, I am about to do a thing in Israel at which the two ears of everyone who hears it will tingle. On that day I will fulfill against Eli all that I have spoken concerning his house, from beginning to end. And I declare to him that I am about to punish his house forever, for the iniquity that he knew, because his sons were blaspheming God, and he did not restrain them. Therefore I swear to the house of Eli that the iniquity of Eli's house shall not be atoned for by sacrifice or offering forever" (1 Samuel 3:11-14 ESV).

Notice how even though God had nothing good to say about Eli, Samuel never left Eli's side. This does not mean we stay under abuse, however, for that's not what God has called us to do-even David fled from Saul. However, I do believe there are times people leave churches before God intended for them to do so.

Samuel's obedience led to him growing, and the Lord was with him. The Bible says,

> "And Samuel grew, and the Lord was with him and let none of his words fall to the ground. And all Israel from Dan to Beersheba knew that Samuel was established as a prophet of the Lord. And the Lord appeared again at Shiloh, for the Lord revealed himself to Samuel at Shiloh by the word of the Lord" (1 Samuel 3:19-21 ESV).

God let none of Samuel's words fall to the ground! This means that when he interceded or declared God's word, he had God's complete backing. The word "Shiloh" foreshadows the Messiah. Jacob stated, "The scepter will not depart from Judah, nor the staff from between his feet, until Shiloh comes and the allegiance of the nations is his" (Genesis 49:10 BSB).

The Lord appearing to Samuel at Shiloh could also mean for us today that it's in the presence of Jesus that we encounter God. Lastly, God showed up to Samuel through His Word. All intercessors must know the Word of God to discern the heart of God.

Samuel didn't just become an intercessor in one day-
he had to grow into it. In the next section, we will talk about
Samuel the intercessor. As we discuss his interceding heart,
remember his intercession was built on: staying in the house
of God (fellowshipping with the believers), near the presence
of God (1 Samuel 3:3), and submitting to the man of God he
was placed under.

Samuel The Intercessor

After the death of Eli, Samuel took over as the final
judge of Israel. He pursued God and it impacted the nation of
Israel as a whole. Prior to this, God's judgment came on all
of Israel.

The judgment of Israel took place because of Eli's
children's disobedience and Eli's reluctance to discipline
them. God had called Eli's family to stand in the gap for the
nation, but instead, they decided to neglect their duty as
intercessors. This resulted in a spiritual death which
manifested in the natural. As a result, Eli and his sons died
along with many others in the land of Israel.

Following the death of Eli, something else transpired
which prophetically described the situation.

"His daughter-in-law, the wife of Phinehas, was pregnant and near the time of delivery. When she heard the news that the ark of God had been captured and that her father-in-law and her husband were dead, she went into labor and gave birth, but was overcome by her labor pains. As she was dying, the women attending her said, 'Don't despair; you have given birth to a son.' But she did not respond or pay any attention. She named the boy Ichabod, saying, 'The Glory has departed from Israel'—because of the capture of the ark of God and the deaths of her father-in-law and her husband. She said, 'The Glory has departed from Israel, for the ark of God has been captured'" (1 Samuel 4:19-22).

Eli's negligence led to the glory of God departing. After God allowed the Ark of the Covenant to be taken by the Philistines, no one from Israel attempted to go rescue it from the enemy. God, being full of mercy, waged war against the Philistines, broke their idol Dagon, and afflicted the Philistine people (1 Samuel 5).

God was still fighting Israel's enemies even after Israel had abandoned Him. Eventually, the Philistines could no longer handle the affliction that was placed on them by God because they stole the ark of the covenant, so they placed the ark of covenant on a cart, and had the cart be carried by two cows (1 Samuel 6:7-8). They said,

"...keep watching it. If it goes up to its own territory, toward Beth Shemesh, then the Lord has brought this great disaster on us. But if it does not, then we will know that it was not his hand that struck us but that it happened to us by chance" (1 Samuel 6:9).

The cows carried the cart with the Ark of the Covenant all the way to Beth Shemesh. No one led the presence of God back to Israel, and no Israelite went to rescue the ark of God, yet God still fought against Israel's enemies and pursued Israel even though they turned their backs on Him. God is always pursuing us!

This is a great example of the kindness of God. While yet we were sinners, Christ died for us (Romans 5:8). Yet, His kindness is meant to lead us to repentance (Romans 2:4).

Samuel called the whole nation back to repentance. As intercessors, we too should seek to call our city, nation, and world back to repentance. The calling of the people back to repentance must be driven by an understanding that God is pursuing the world like He pursued the Israelites.

"So the men of Kiriath Jearim came and took up the ark of the Lord. They brought it to Abinadab's house on the hill and consecrated Eleazar his son to guard the ark of the Lord. The ark remained at Kiriath Jearim a long time—twenty years in all. Then all the people of Israel turned back to the Lord.

So Samuel said to all the Israelites, "If you are returning to the Lord with all your hearts, then rid yourselves of the foreign gods and the Ashtoreths and commit yourselves to the Lord and serve him only, and he will deliver you out of the hand of the Philistines." So the Israelites put away their Baals and Ashtoreths, and served the Lord only. Then Samuel said, "Assemble all Israel at Mizpah, and I will intercede with the Lord for you." When they had assembled at Mizpah, they drew water and poured it out before the Lord. On that day they fasted and there they confessed, "We have sinned against the Lord." Now Samuel was serving as leader of Israel at Mizpah" (1 Samuel 7:1-6).

In verses 5 and 6 of this passage, we read that the people "drew water and poured it out before the Lord." The drawing of the water and pouring it out symbolizes their wholehearted pursuit of God. This wholehearted pursuit is also shown in their fasting.

As intercessors, we must teach people how to pour out their souls to God like the children of Israel poured the water out on the ground. Like the children of Israel fasted and confessed their sins to God, the church must seek God with similar desperation. It is only after we get desperate like this that we will see complete restoration in our land.

After this time of intercession, Israel's enemies, the Philistines, attacked Israel. The children of Israel were terrified and said to Samuel,

> "Do not stop crying out to the Lord our God for us, that he may rescue us from the hand of the Philistines." Then Samuel took a suckling lamb and sacrificed it as a whole burnt offering to the Lord. He cried out to the Lord on Israel's behalf, and the Lord answered him" (1 Samuel 7:8-9).

The Israelites went from always losing battles to becoming victorious over their enemies because God had established an intercessor in the land. Samuel stood in the gap for the children of Israel and God fought on their behalf.

> "While Samuel was sacrificing the burnt offering, the Philistines drew near to engage Israel in battle. But that day the Lord thundered with loud thunder against the Philistines and threw them into such a panic that they were routed before the Israelites" (1 Samuel 7:10).

This is the power of intercession. The Philistines did not invade Israel's territory again during the lifetime of Samuel. Proceeding this victory, Samuel took a stone and set it up between Mizpah and Shen. Then, he named the stone Ebenezer, meaning *the Lord is my helper.*

Mizpah means "the watchtower".[10] It's at the place known as a watchtower that Samuel assumes leadership over the children of Israel. A watchtower is a high tower where a sentinel watches for enemies, forest fires, etc.[11] Without watchtowers, a kingdom or city can easily be breached because they don't see the enemy coming. It's one of the most important parts of a castle.

Spiritually, when we intercede, we become watchmen in the watchtower. Eli and his children neglected the watchtower and because of this the city was ransacked. Samuel re-established the watchtower of intercession, and because of this, God became Israel's Ebenezer (helper) again.

Samuel believed so much in intercession that he equated not interceding with sinning. He said, "as for me, far be it from me that I should sin against the Lord by failing to pray for you. And I will teach you the way that is good and right" (1 Samuel 12:23). A true intercessor must view intercession as Samuel did.

CHAPTER 11 QUESTIONS

1. What are the three things Samuel did? Why is it important for intercessors to follow Samuel's example?

2. God may call us, but it is our job to
   _____.

3. What makes our response to God easier?

4. Many people are quick to leave a church or ministry because they are hurt or see something better. List two reasons that would justify you leaving a ministry or church.

5. What should call people to repentance be driven by?

CHAPTER 12

Biblical Intercessors: Jesus

As the children of Israel continued in sin, even after God had been patient with them and forgiven them, God spoke to Ezekiel and told him that even if Noah, Daniel, and Job were there, "their righteousness would save no one but themselves" (Ezekiel 14:14 NLT). Noah, who is mentioned first, was the first to deal with a world that was completely overcome by their sinful ways.

When Noah was between 500-600 years old, God told him to build an ark because He was going to flood the earth (Genesis 5:32; 6; 7). In 2 Peter 2:5, we find that God protected Noah, a preacher of righteousness, and seven others. Noah's righteousness and intercession helped save his family from destruction (Genesis 7:1).

Noah was a righteous man who preached to the world, and we can rightfully assume he was an intercessor. His interceding heart can be seen after the flood was over when he, on his own accord, sacrificed to God. God never told him to sacrifice clean animals- he did it himself, which means that he had been doing it before.

> "Then Noah built an altar to the Lord and, taking some of all the clean animals and clean birds, he sacrificed burnt offerings on it. The Lord smelled the pleasing aroma and said in his heart: "Never again will I curse the ground because of humans, even though every inclination of the human heart is evil from childhood. And never again will I destroy all living creatures, as I have done. "As long as the earth endures, seedtime and harvest, cold and heat, summer and winter, day and night will never cease" (Genesis 8:20-22).

Noah was a blameless and righteous man in his generation. He preached the truth to the lost and interceded. But we still read that his righteousness would only save himself from God's judgment in Ezekiel 14.

After Noah, God mentions Daniel. Daniel, at the time of Ezekiel, is writing his book. He is a young man, yet his righteous acts are known by many.

There is much written about Daniel's intercessions. In Daniel 2, his intercessory prayers saved his friends and the wise men of Babylon. Then in chapter 9, Daniel intercedes for the whole nation of Israel, reminding God of his words through the prophet Jeremiah:

""…When seventy years are completed for Babylon, I will come to you and fulfill my good promise to bring you back to this place. For I know the plans I have for you,' declares the Lord, 'plans to prosper you and not to harm you, plans to give you hope and a future. Then you will call on me and come and pray to me, and I will listen to you. You will seek me and find me when you seek me with all your heart. I will be found by you,' declares the Lord, 'and will bring you back from captivity. I will gather you from all the nations and places where I have banished you,' declares the Lord, 'and will bring you back to the place from which I carried you into exile'" (Jeremiah 29:10-14).

Daniel, being the great intercessor he was, knew the words God spoke through Jeremiah the prophet. When the 70 years were upon the children of Israel, Daniel repented for the sins of his people and cried out to God for deliverance (Daniel 9). His intercession was heard, an angel showed up, and Israel's deliverance began (Daniel 9:20-21).

Daniel is the true definition of a prayer warrior. According to Scripture, Daniel prayed regularly three times a day (Daniel 6:10-28). If there was anyone who could intercede for the children of Israel and cause the wrath of God to be appeased, one would think it would be Daniel. However, even Daniel could not save Israel from the impending doom mentioned by Ezekiel because of their national sin.

Last on the list was the righteous man by the name of Job whose righteousness was boasted about by God Himself (Job 1). Job interceded for his whole family on a regular basis, going as far as sacrificing on their behalf just in case they sinned (Job 1:5). Through his intercession his friends who acted foolishly were delivered from the consequences of their folly (Job 42:8-10).

But just as the other two on this list of righteous men, Jobs' intercessions still would not be able to save Israel. The punishment for sin is death, and although Noah, Daniel, and Job were righteous, they were not sinless. Since men are beset with weaknesses, there came a point where the wrath of God could not be held at bay by mere men. This all changed in the New Testament when Jesus came into the scene. Jesus was perfect in every way and was a Priest, not in the order of man, but in the order of Melchizedek.

> "and Abraham gave him a tenth of everything. First, the name Melchizedek means "king of righteousness"; then also, "king of Salem" means "king of peace." Without father or mother, without genealogy, without beginning of days or end of life, resembling the Son of God, he remains a priest forever" (Hebrews 7:2-3).

Melchizedek, therefore, is a shadowy image in the Old Testament of a future Christ. Many scholars call this a Christophany-an occurrence of the preincarnate Christ in the Old Testament.

Jesus came in the order of this priest who was devoid of sin. "Therefore, he is able to save completely those who come to God through him, because he always lives to intercede for them" (Hebrews 7:25). Unlike Noah, Daniel, Job and any other Old Testament man, Jesus does not need to repent of sin.

This is why, when he intercedes, it is a greater level of intercession and He is "…able to keep you from stumbling and to present you before his glorious presence without fault and with great joy—" (Jude 1:24). What does this mean for us today?

This means we can confidently intercede because of what Jesus did on the cross!

> "Therefore, since we have a great high priest who has ascended into heaven, Jesus the Son of God, let us hold firmly to the faith we profess. For we do not have a high priest who is unable to empathize with our weaknesses, but we have one who has been tempted in every way, just as we are—yet he did not sin. Let us then approach God's throne of grace with confidence, so that we may receive mercy and find

grace to help us in our time of need" (Hebrews 4:14-16).

Jesus has experienced our pain, bore our sin, and ascended into Heaven. Because of this, we can come boldly to God in prayer!

What's stopping you from praying for your nation? Is it sin? Then confess your sin and Jesus will cleanse you. For the Bible says, "If we confess our sins, he is faithful and just and will forgive us our sins and purify us from all unrighteousness" (1 John 1:9).

I can understand why people in the Old Testament were unable to intercede at times. They only had the blood of bulls and goats, so they couldn't fully enter the Holy of Holies. Isaiah says, "All of us have become like one who is unclean, and all our righteous acts are like filthy rags; we all shrivel up like a leaf, and like the wind our sins sweep us away" (Isaiah 64:6). Included in the "all" Isaiah talks about are Noah, Daniel, and Job.

Although righteous, these three men were limited in their intercession because it was based on their righteousness. They had God *with* them; we have God *in* us! His Spirit intercedes through us. "In the same way, the Spirit helps us in our weakness. We do not know what we ought to pray for, but the Spirit himself intercedes for us through wordless groans" (Romans 8:26).

Through his righteousness and intercession, Noah saved future generations here on earth, but he could not save them from their eternal damnation. Likewise, Daniel, through his intercession, helped rescue his friends, saved the wisemen of Babylon, and even started the restoration process for Israel. Yet again, his intercession couldn't bring forth spiritual salvation.

Lastly, Job, who was righteous and blameless, still would fall short if he was asked to intercede for someone's soul to be saved. As great as these intercessors were, their intercession was limited because they did not have Christ living in them. But since we have Christ living in us and His Spirit praying through us, people's spirits can be set free from the bondage of sin when we intercede. We can even snatch some people out of prison (Jude 1:20-23).

So what are you waiting for? The Bible says, "…The effectual fervent prayer of a righteous man availeth much" (James 5:16 KJV). Elijah, who had the same sinful nature we have, prayed earnestly in the Old Testament that it would not rain, and it did not rain for 3 years and 6 months. Then he prayed again that it would rain, and it did (James 5:17-18).

Elijah did all this under the Old Covenant without Christ coming and dying and his sins being completely wiped clean. Imagine what would happen if we who are in a better covenant (Hebrews 8:6), we who are now the righteousness of God (2 Corinthians 5:21), we who are called the sons of God (John 1:12-13), start believing we are and praying boldly and passionately like Elijah. How the world would change!

Friend, you are being commissioned today to intercede for your family, friends, city, country, nation, world! Arise intercessor! Pray boldly! Pray effectively! Pray!

CHAPTER 12 QUESTIONS

1. Why couldn't Noah, Daniel, and Job save Israel from the impending wrath of God?

2. Why can we confidently intercede if we're in Christ?

3. Why were people in the Old Testament limited in their intercession?

4. Have you committed yourself to a lifestyle of intercession? Are you ready to answer the call of God to intercede?

SPECIAL THANKS

I would like to thank my spiritual son Gloire Emmanuel Ndongala for helping with the writing process. Mariajose Staley Ramón Ros for editing the Spanish version. Bellarmee Milosi for editing the French version. Kelani Daniels for editing the whole book and for her contribution on the writing process. Lastly, Mark Hunter for all his help.

REFERENCES

1. "What Is the Noun for Intercede?" *WordHippo*. Accessed March 16, 2022. https://www.wordhippo.com/what-is/the-noun-for/intercede.html.

2. Zalani, Rochi. "Average Screen Time: Statistics 2021." *ECM*. Last modified November 5, 2021. Accessed March 16, 2022. https://elitecontentmarketer.com/screen-time-statistics/.

3. *Strong's Greek: 4336. Προσεύχομαι (PROSEUCHOMAI) -- to Pray*. Accessed March 17, 2022. https://biblehub.com/greek/4336.htm.

4. Ibid.

5. Hasa. "Difference between Love and Compassion." *Compare the Difference Between Similar Terms*.

Differencebetween.com, April 4, 2019. Last modified April 4, 2019. Accessed March 17, 2022. https://www.differencebetween.com/difference-between-love-and-compassion/.

6. *Strong's Greek: 4697. Σπλαγχνίζομαι (SPLAGCHNIZOMAI) -- to Be Moved in the Inward Parts, I.e. to Feel Compassion.* Accessed March 17, 2022. https://biblehub.com/greek/4697.htm.

7. *Strong's Hebrew: 1847. דַּעַת (Daath) -- Knowledge.* Accessed March 17, 2022. https://biblehub.com/hebrew/1847.htm.

8. *Genesis 18:21 Commentaries: "I Will Go down Now, and See If They Have Done Entirely According to Its Outcry, Which Has Come to Me; and If Not, I Will Know.".* Accessed March 17, 2022. https://biblehub.com/commentaries/genesis/18-21.htm.

9. "Home." *Bible Study*. Accessed March 17, 2022. https://www.biblestudy.org/meaning-names/zoar-bela.html.

10. Staff, BibleStudyTools. "Mizpah." *Definition and Meaning - Bible Dictionary*. BibleStudyTools, n.d. Accessed March 17, 2022. https://www.biblestudytools.com/dictionary/mizpah/?amp.

11. "Watchtower Definition and Meaning: Collins English Dictionary." *Watchtower Definition and Meaning | Collins English Dictionary*. HarperCollins Publishers Ltd, n.d. Accessed March 16, 2022. https://www.collinsdictionary.com/us/dictionary/english/watchtower.

www.ingramcontent.com/pod-product-compliance
Lightning Source LLC
Chambersburg PA
CBHW072356090426
42741CB00012B/3051